E A S Y   P I A N O
RICHARD CLAYDERMAN
C O L L E C T I O N

T0084229

A Joint
Publication
of

ARC
MUSIC GROUP

Music
Publishers,
New York,
New York

and

HAL•LEONARD®
CORPORATION
7777 W. BLUEMOUND RD. P.O. BOX 13819 MILWAUKEE, WI 53213

Dear Friend,

Perhaps you are a beginning piano student or someone who plays well but has difficulty finding the time to practice. You admire the pleasing and romantic melodies found in the music of Richard Clayderman, but are intimidated by the thought of attempting to play this intricate music yourself on the piano.

The Richard Clayderman Easy Piano Collection has been designed to dispel any feelings of intimidation that you may have had about playing this beautiful music in the past. This book will enable you to accurately recreate Richard Clayderman's style of playing in the easiest way possible.

All of the songs in this collection have been specially arranged to avoid technical difficulties, yet sound full and complete:

- When necessary, the key of the song has been changed from that of the original.
- Some of the melodic lines played in the right hand, as well as several accompaniment patterns for the left hand, have been simplified.
- Fingering, dynamics, and tempo indications are clearly indicated throughout the collection.
- Preliminary exercises that focus on the specific needs of a song are given before most of the songs in the collection. Practice these exercises carefully and you will not only be able to play the song much better, but you will also learn it much faster.

Because of these special features, the **Richard Clayderman Easy Piano Collection** will help you to achieve excellent results quickly and easily. We hope that the time that you spend learning and playing these songs will be as enjoyable for you as listening to the recordings.

EASY PIANO

RICHARD CLAYDERMAN

COLLECTION

CONTENTS

WALK IN THE WOODS

Musique de: Paul de SENNEVILLE
et Olivier TOUSSAINT

Exercises For The Right Hand

Exercise For The Left Hand

Valse lente

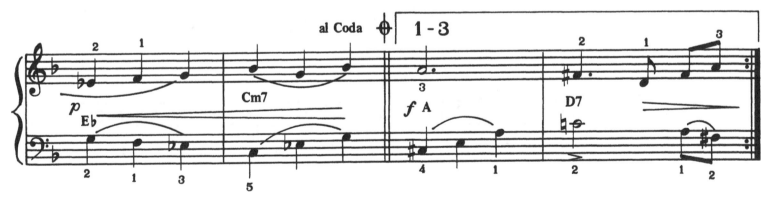

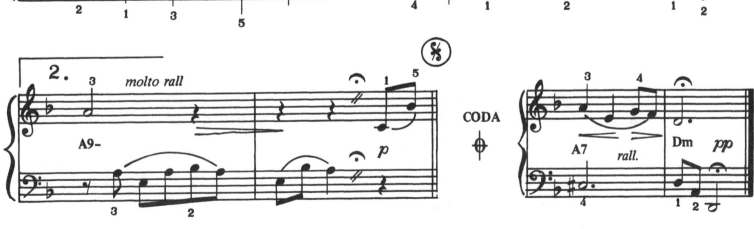

BRAHMS' LULLABY

Musique de: Johannes BRAHMS

Arrangement de: Olivier TOUSSAINT
et Gérard SALESSES

Exercises For The Right Hand

Exercises For The Left Hand

Lento

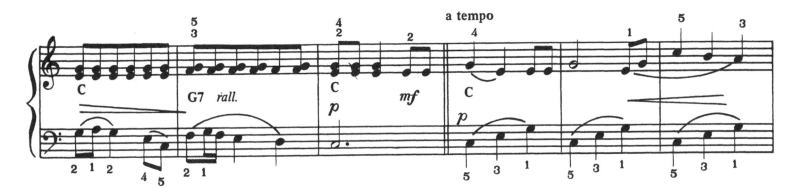

ODE TO JOY

Musique de: Ludwig van BEETHOVEN

Arrangement de: Olivier TOUSSAINT
et Gérard SALESSES

Exercise For The Right Hand

Andante

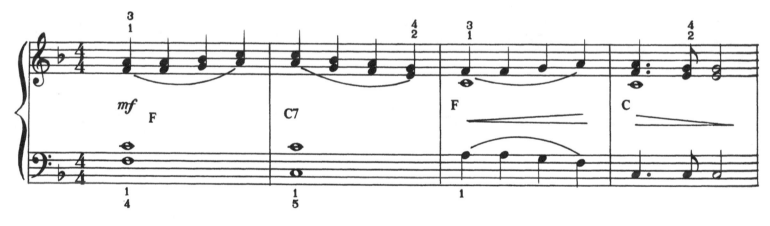

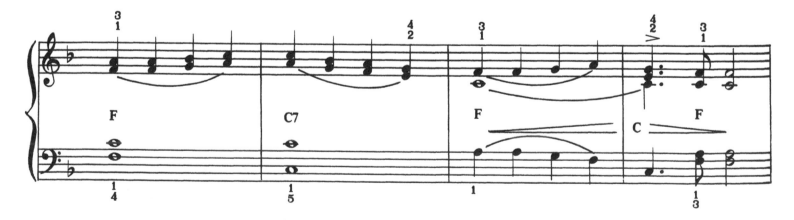

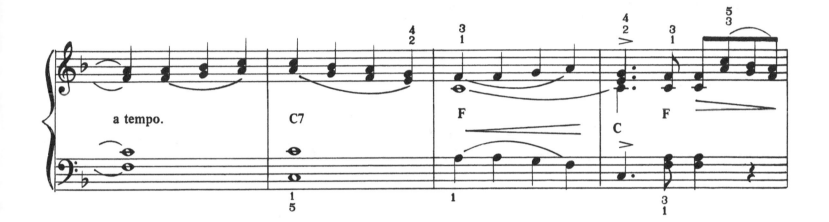

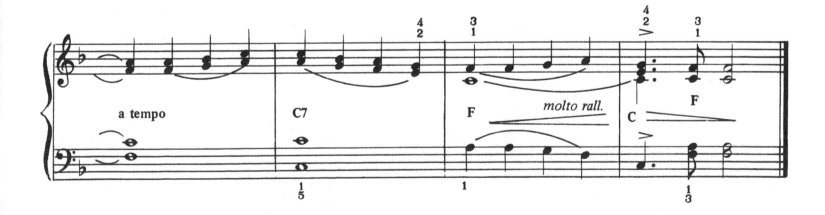

SECRET GARDEN

Musique de
Paul de SENNEVILLE

Exercise For The Right Hand

Exercise For The Left Hand

Moderato

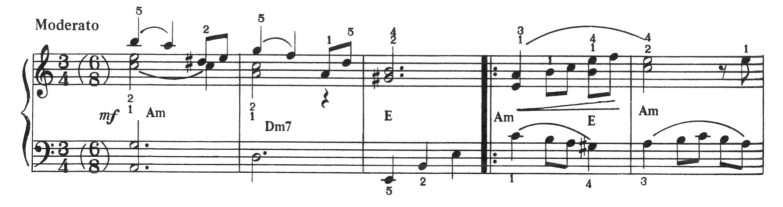

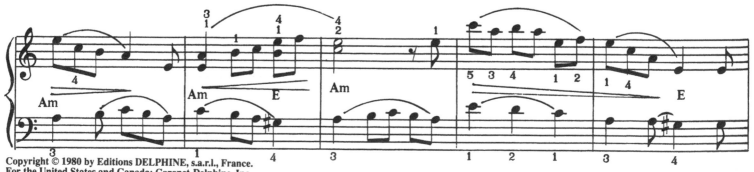

Tous droits réservés
pour tous pays

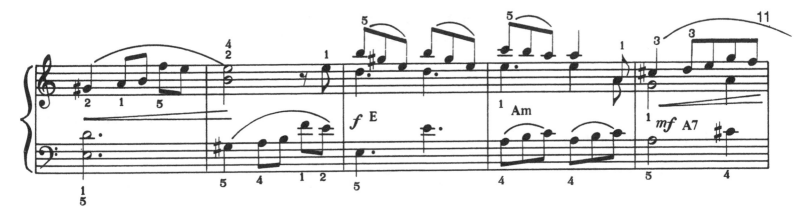

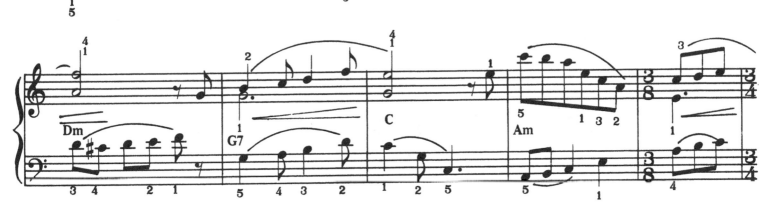

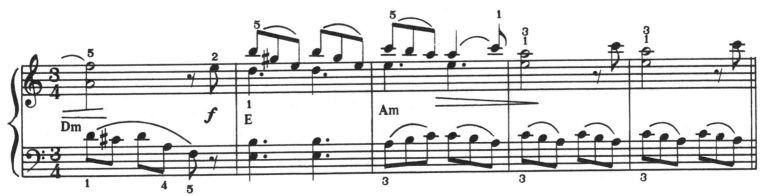

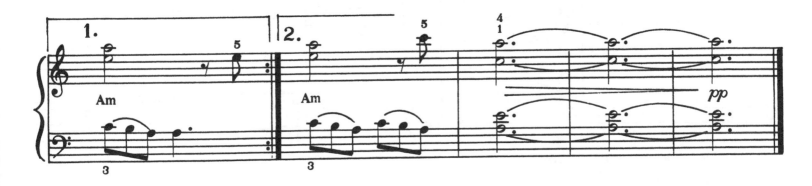

MURMURS

Musique de
Paul de SENNEVILLE

Exercise For The Right Hand

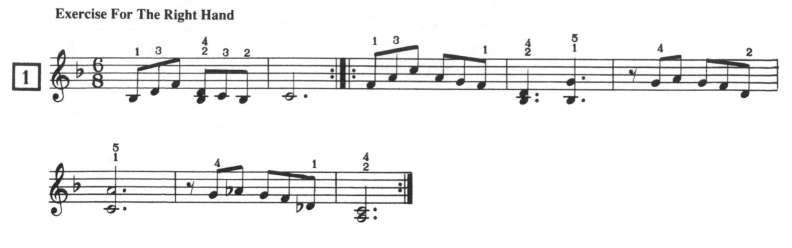

Exercise For The Left Hand

Lento

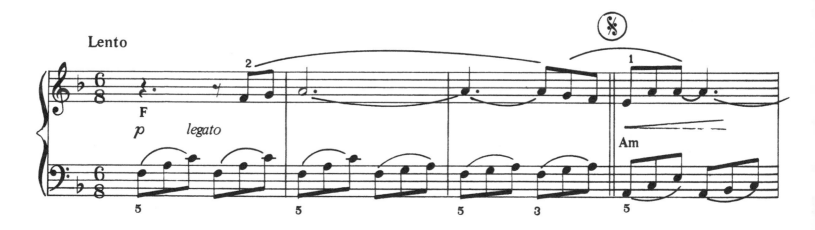

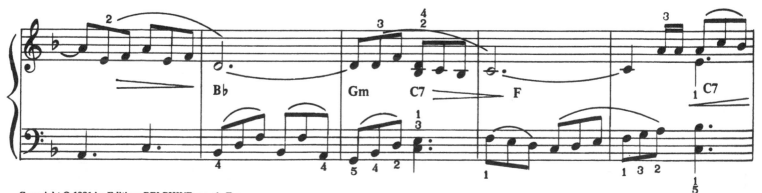

Tous droits résevés
pour tous pays

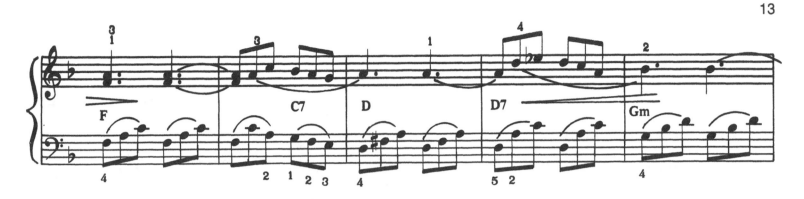

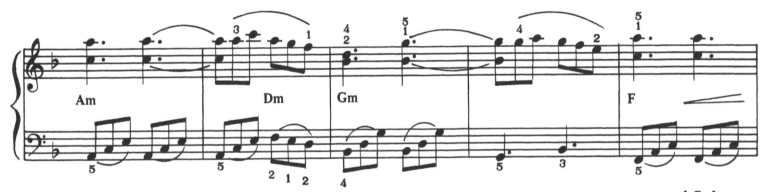

ELEANA

Musique de:
Paul de SENNEVILLE

Tous droits réservés
pour tous pays.

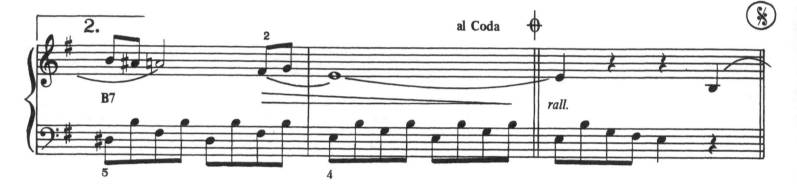

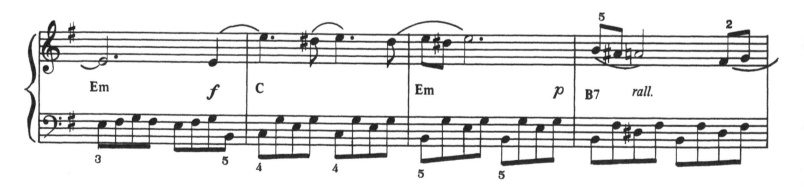

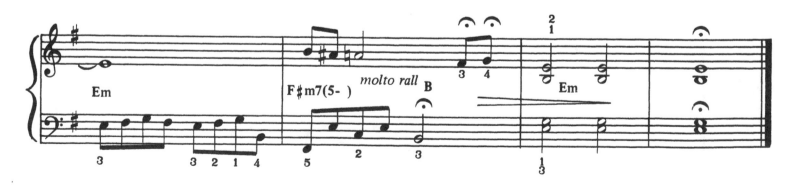

LIEBESTRAUM

Musique de: Franz LISZT

Arrangement de: Olivier TOUSSAINT
et Gérard SALESSES

Exercise For The Right Hand

Exercise For The Left Hand

Moderato

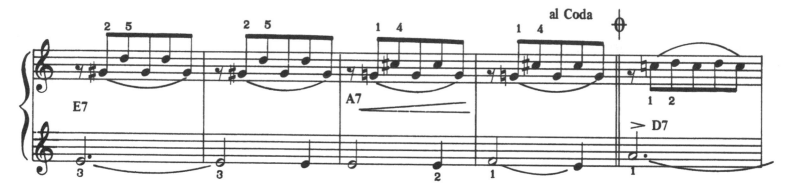

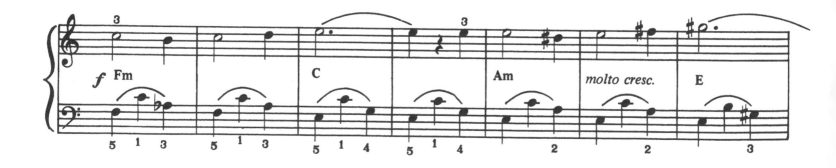

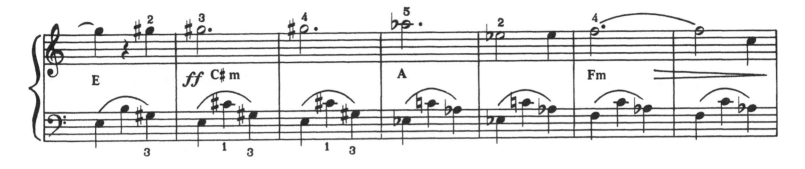

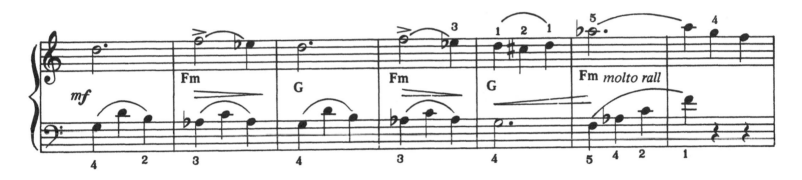

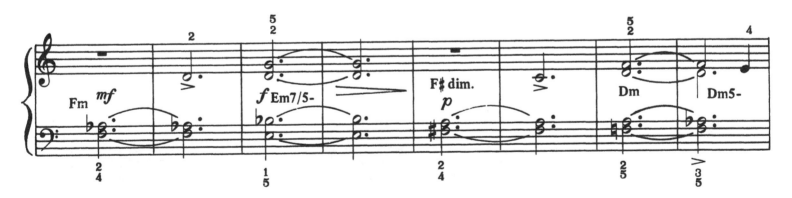

CHOPIN'S ETUDE, OP. 12, NO. 3
Musique de: F. CHOPIN

Arrangement de: Olivier TOUSSAINT
et Gérard SALESSES

Exercises For The Right Hand

Exercise For The Left Hand

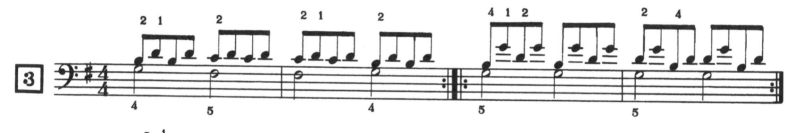

Andante

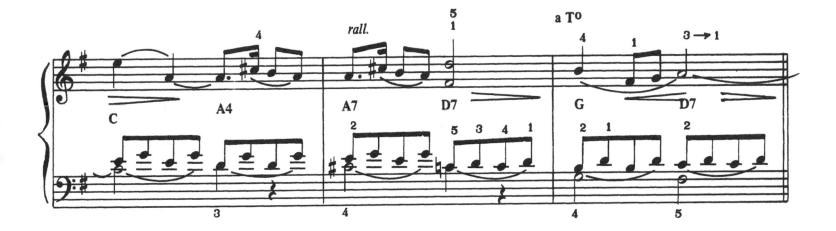

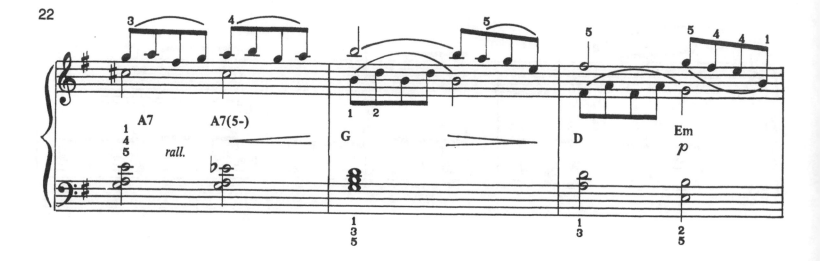

L FOR LOVE

Musique de: Paul de SENNEVILLE
et Olivier TOUSSAINT

Exercises For The Right Hand

Exercise For The Left Hand

Moderato

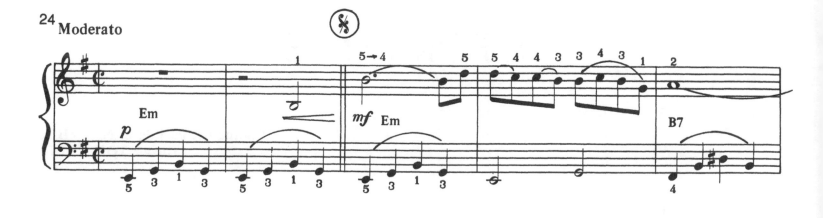

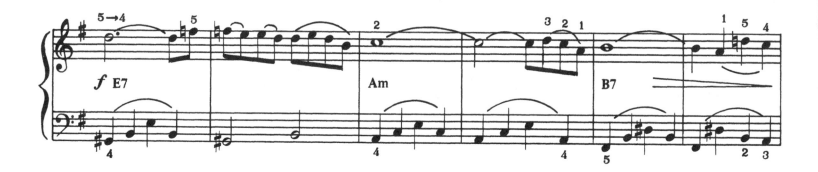

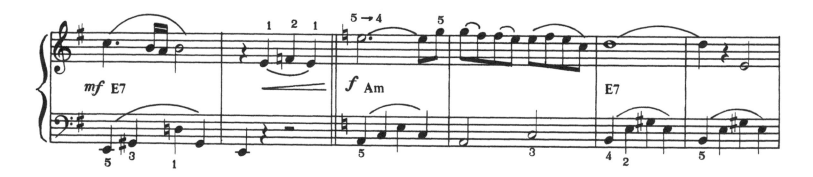

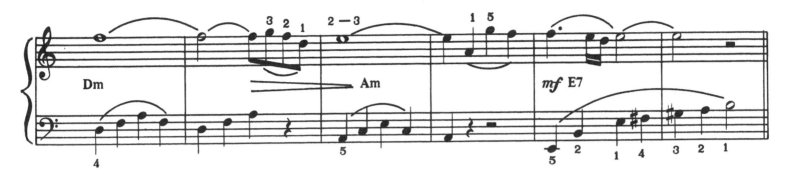

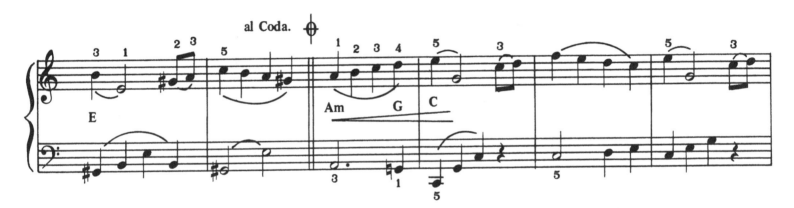

DIVA

Musique de: Paul de SENNEVILLE
et Jean BAUDLOT

Exercise For The Right Hand

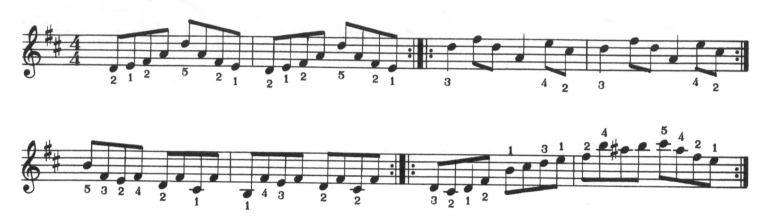

Exercise For The Left Hand

Allegro

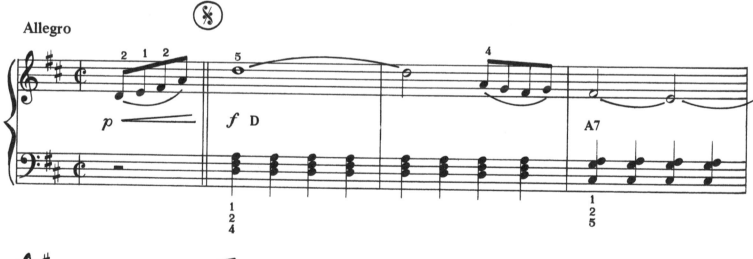

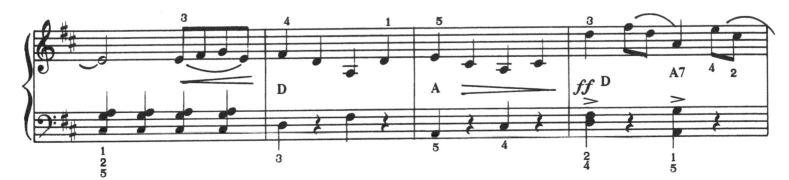

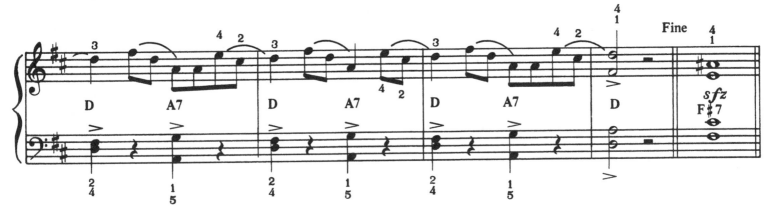

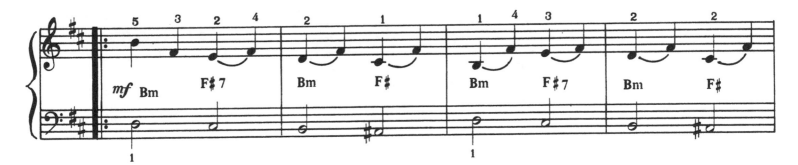

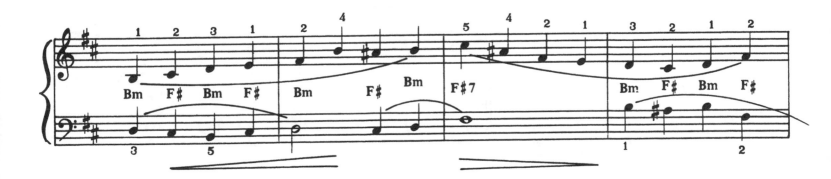

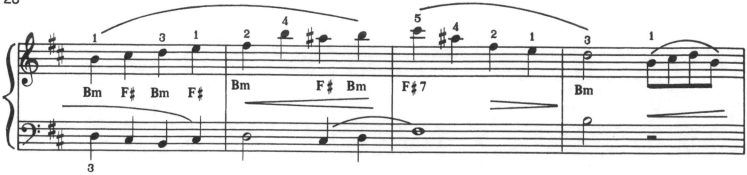

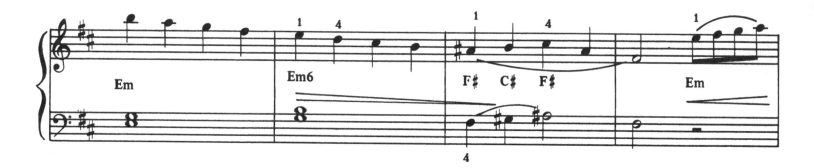

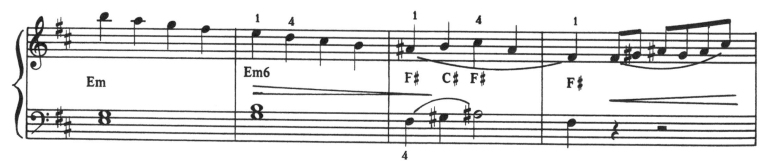

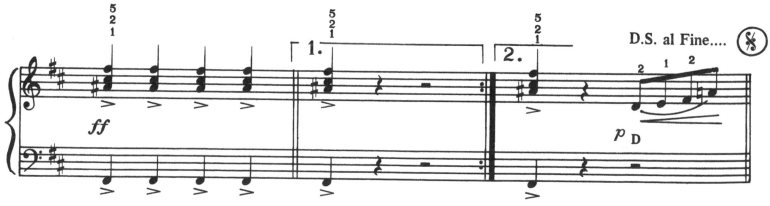

FRAGILE HEART

Musique de: Paul de SENNEVILLE
et Jean BAUDLOT

Exercise For The Right Hand

Moderato

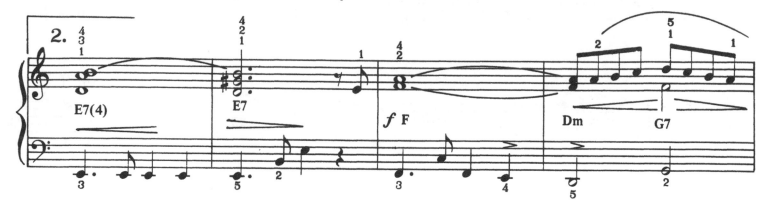

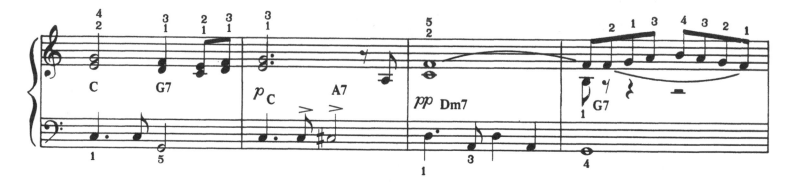

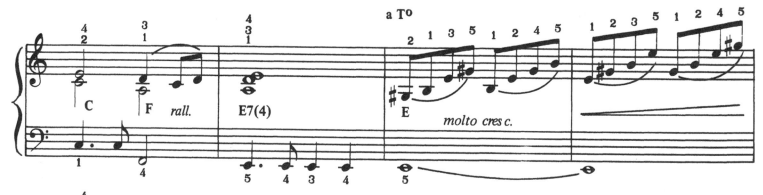

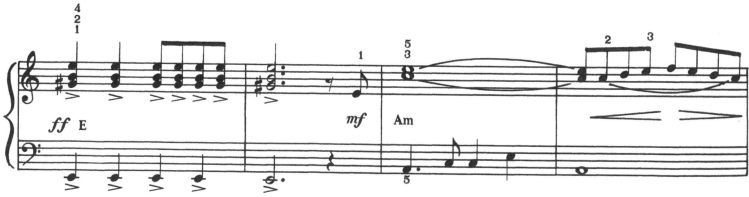

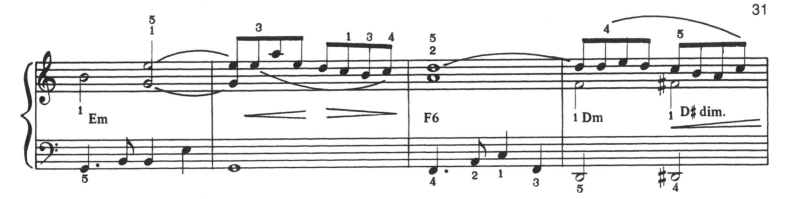

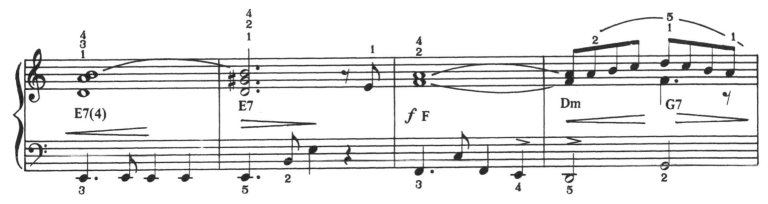

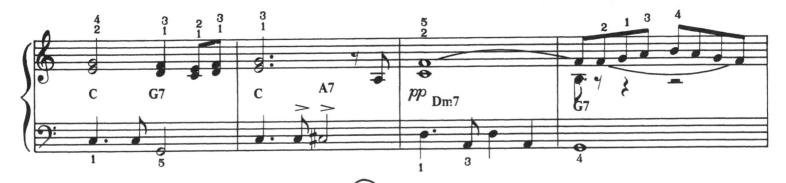

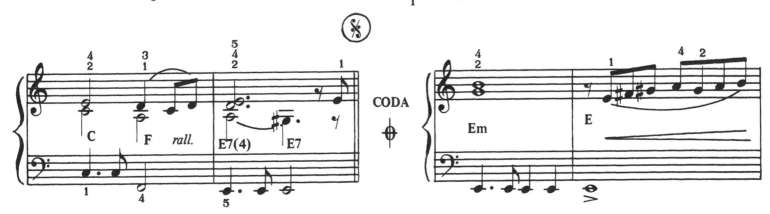

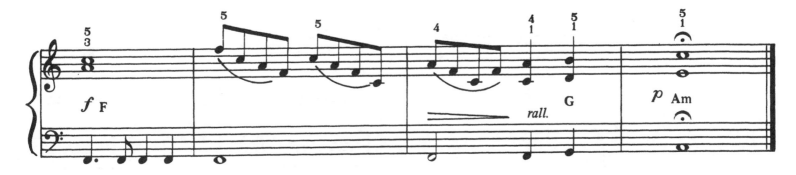

LYPHARD MELODY

Musique de: Paul de SENNEVILLE
et Olivier TOUSSAINT

Exercises For The Right Hand

Exercise For The Left Hand

Slow

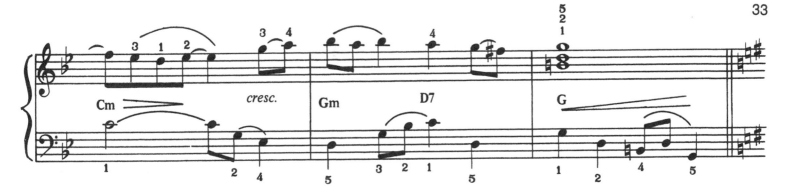

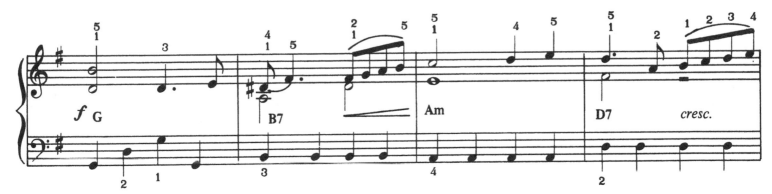

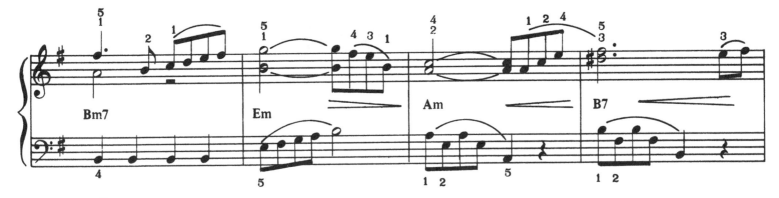

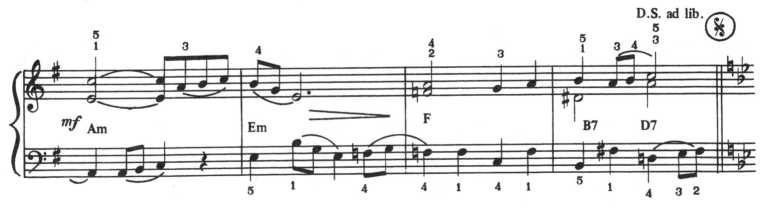

FÜR ELISE

Musique de: Ludwig van BEETHOVEN

Arrangement de: Olivier TOUSSAINT
et Gérard SALESSES

Exercise For The Right Hand

Tous droits réservés
pour tous pays

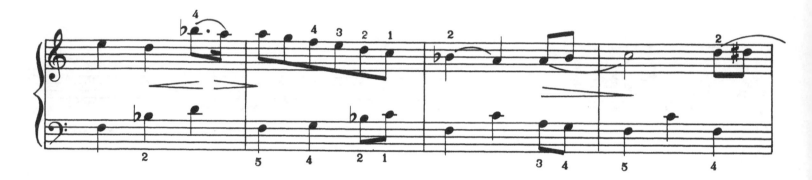

CODA

SAD HEART

Musique de:
Paul de SENNEVILLE

Exercice For The Right Hand

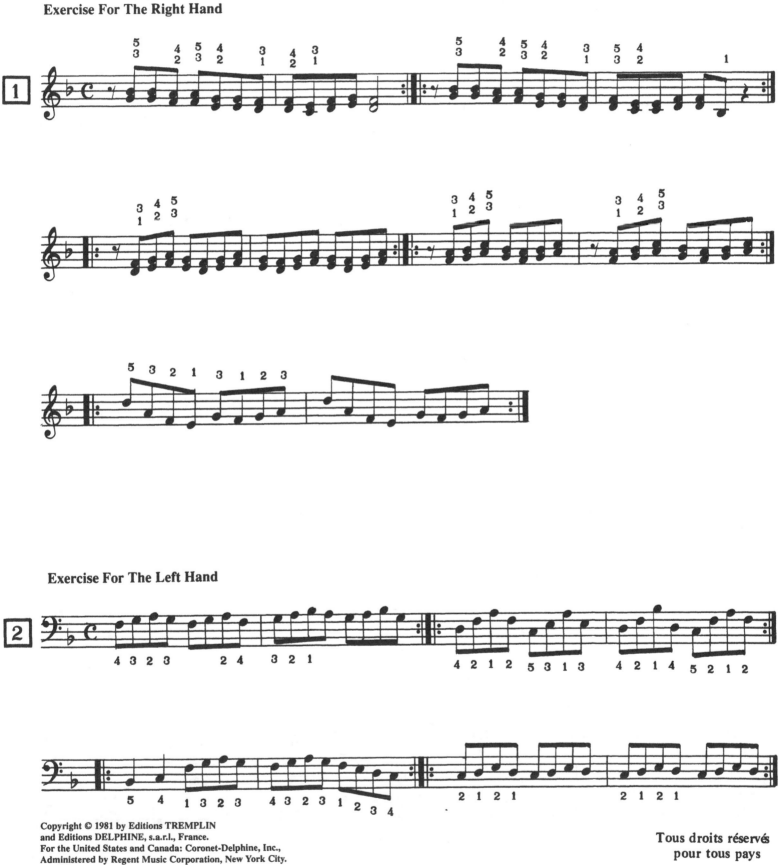

Exercise For The Left Hand

Tous droits réservés
pour tous pays

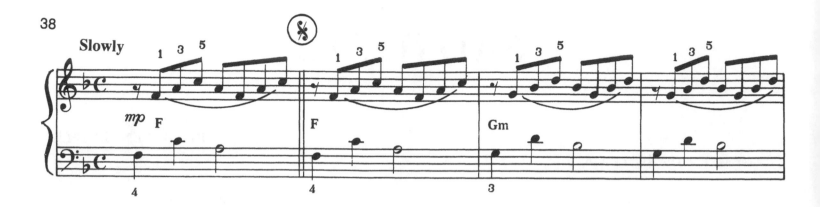

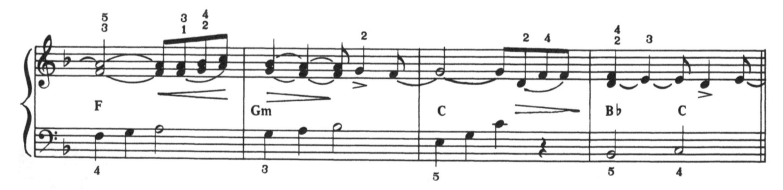

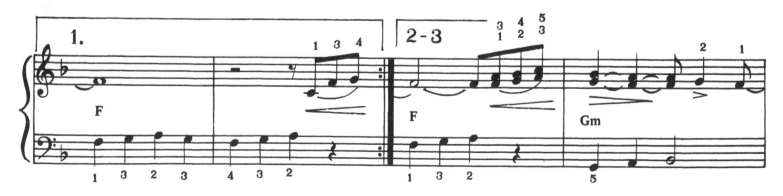

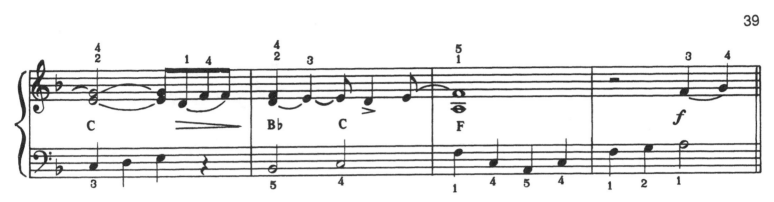

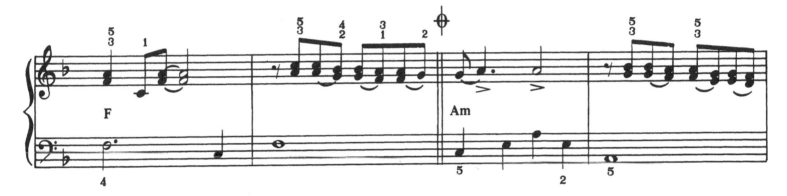

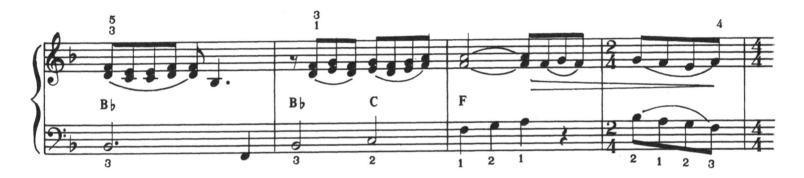

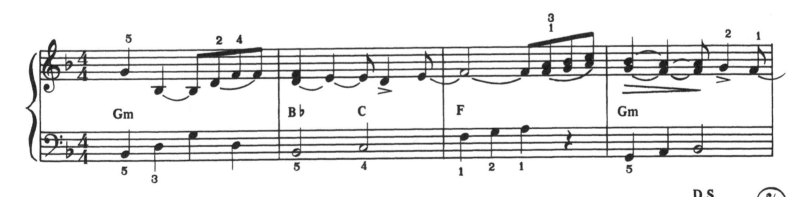

D.S.
al Coda 𝄋

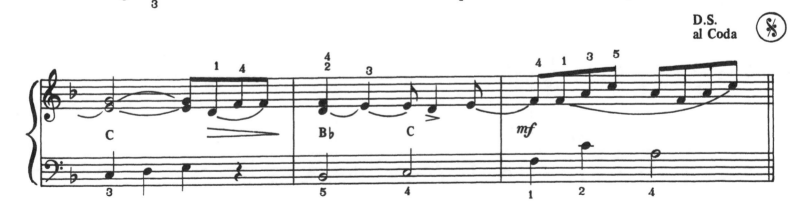

CODA

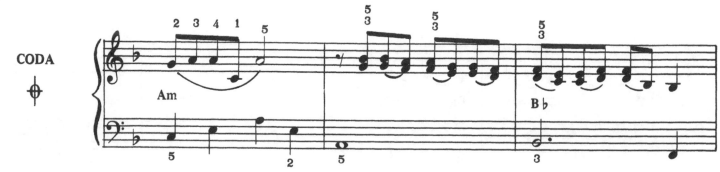

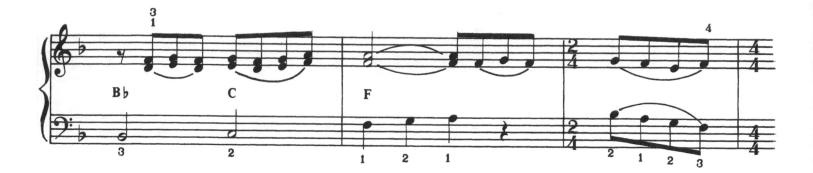

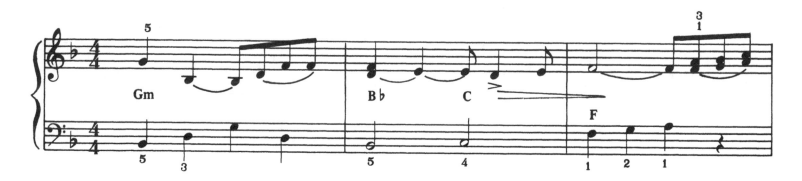

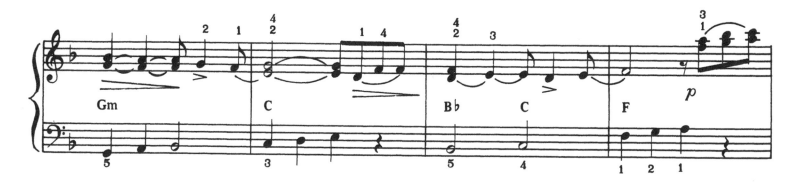

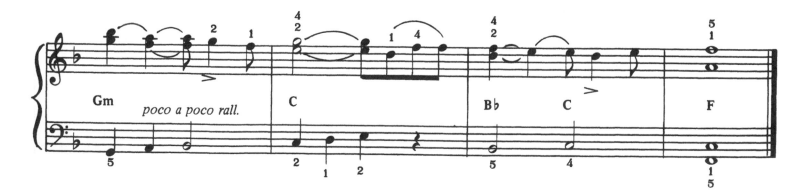

poco a poco rall.

AVE MARIA

Musique de: BACH—GOUNOD

Arrangement de: Olivier TOUSSAINT
et Gérard SALESSES

Allegro moderato

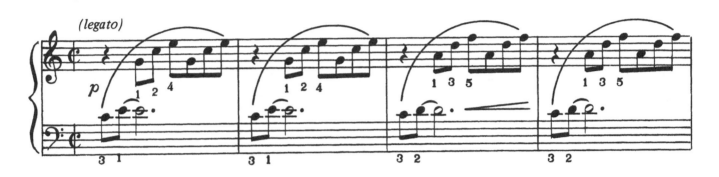

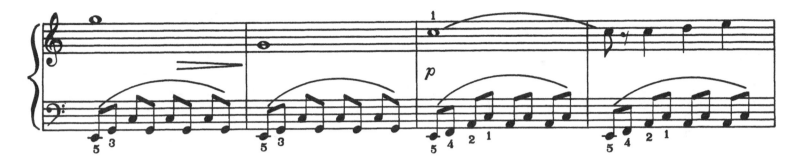

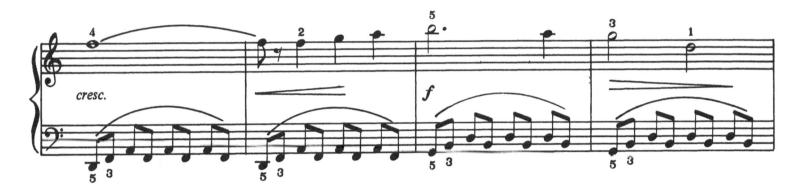

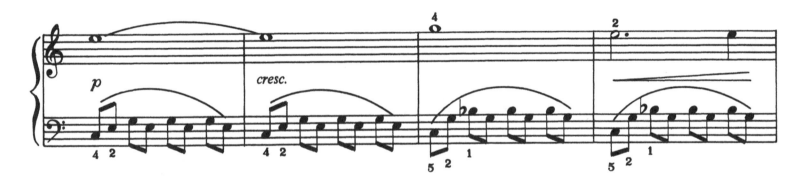

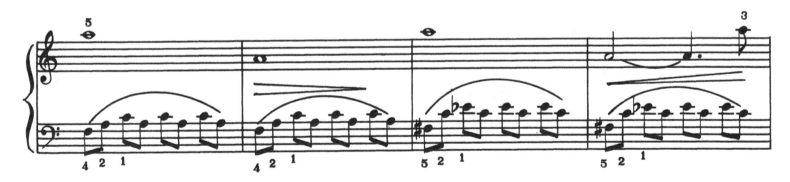

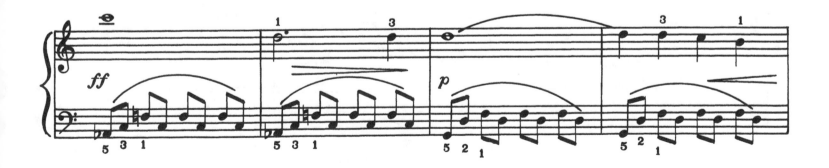

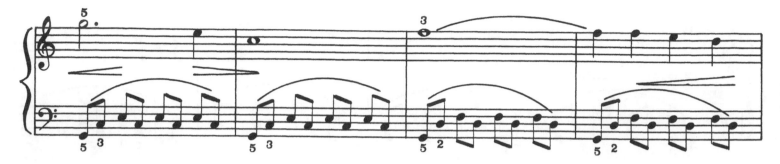

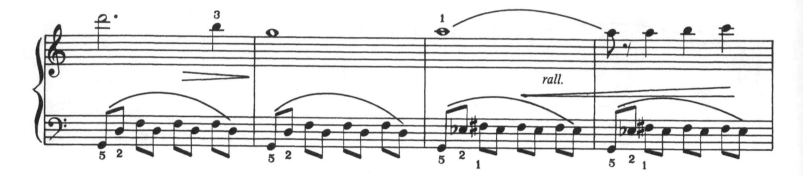

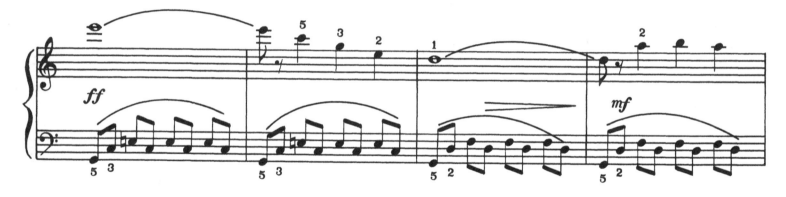

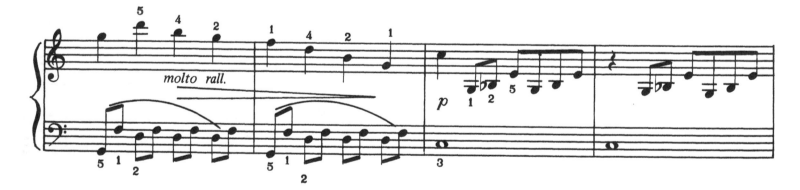

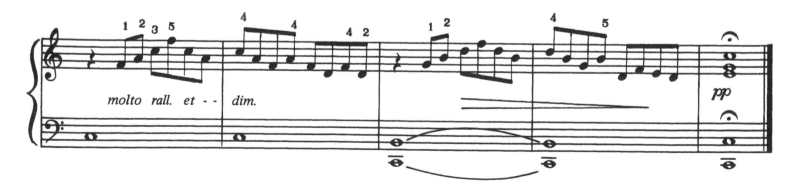

BARCAROLLE

Musique de: J. OFFENBACH

Arrangement de: Olivier TOUSSAINT
et Gérard SALESSES

Exercise For The Right Hand

Exercise For The Left Hand

Moderato

a tempo

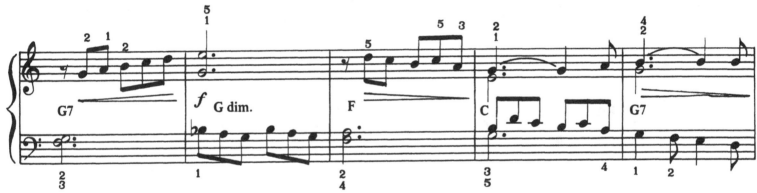

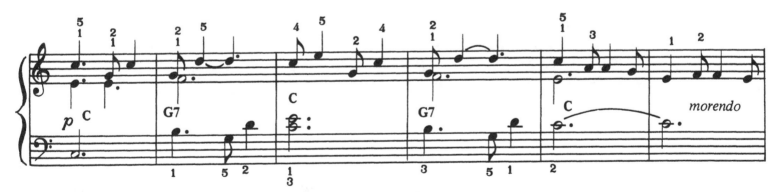

THE OCEAN

Musique de:
Olivier TOUSSAINT

Exercise For The Right Hand

Exercise For The Left Hand

Slowly

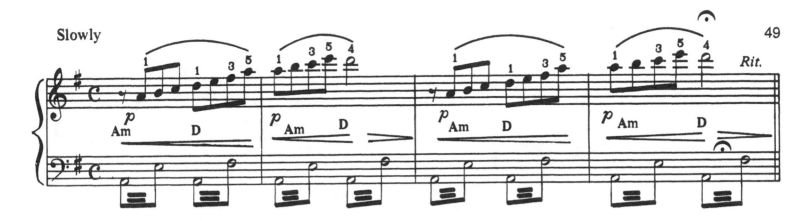

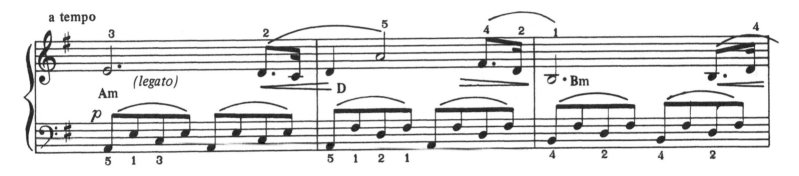

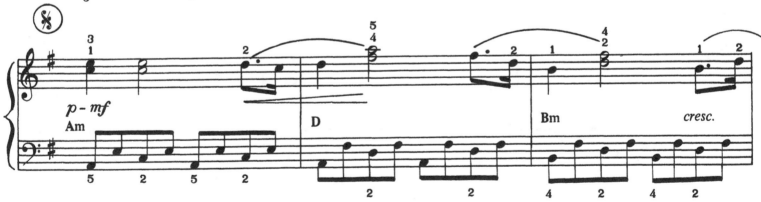

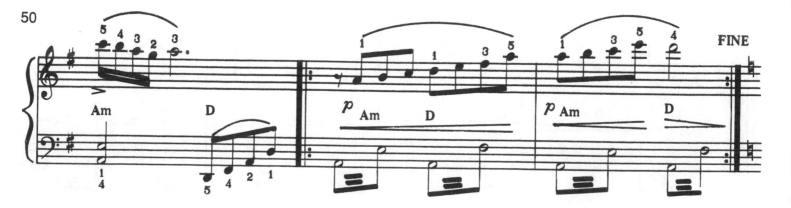

FINE

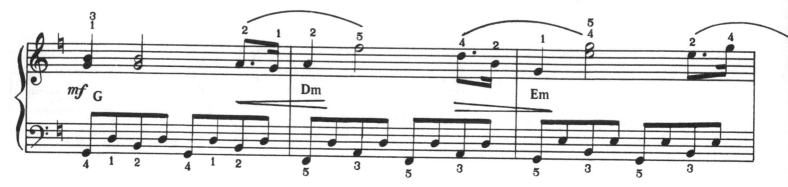

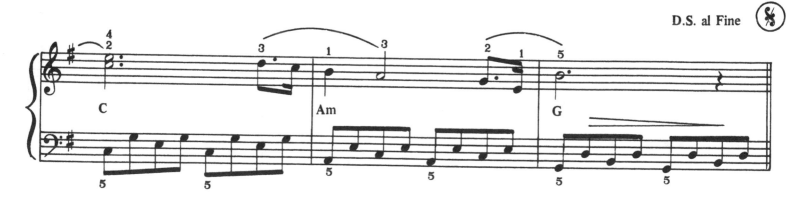

D.S. al Fine

LADY "DI"

Music by Paul de Senneville and Jean Baudlot
Words by Olivier Toussaint

Fairly bright tempo

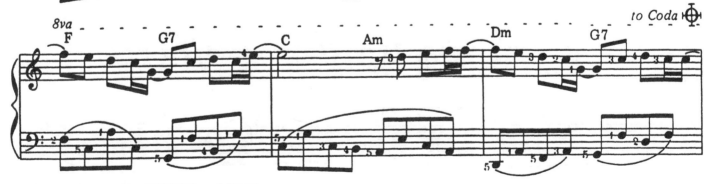

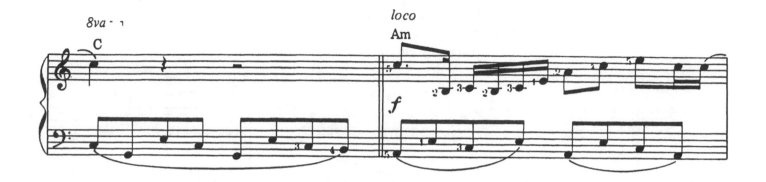

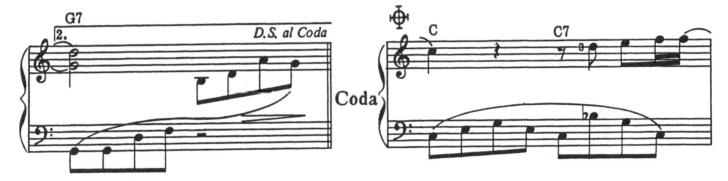

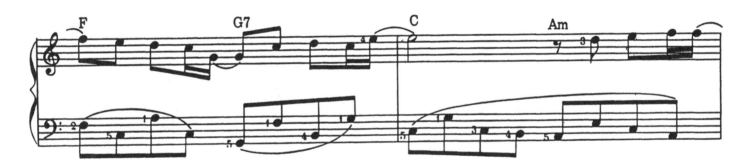

BALLADE POUR ADELINE

Musique de: Paul de SENNEVILLE
et Olivier TOUSSAINT

Exercises For The Right Hand

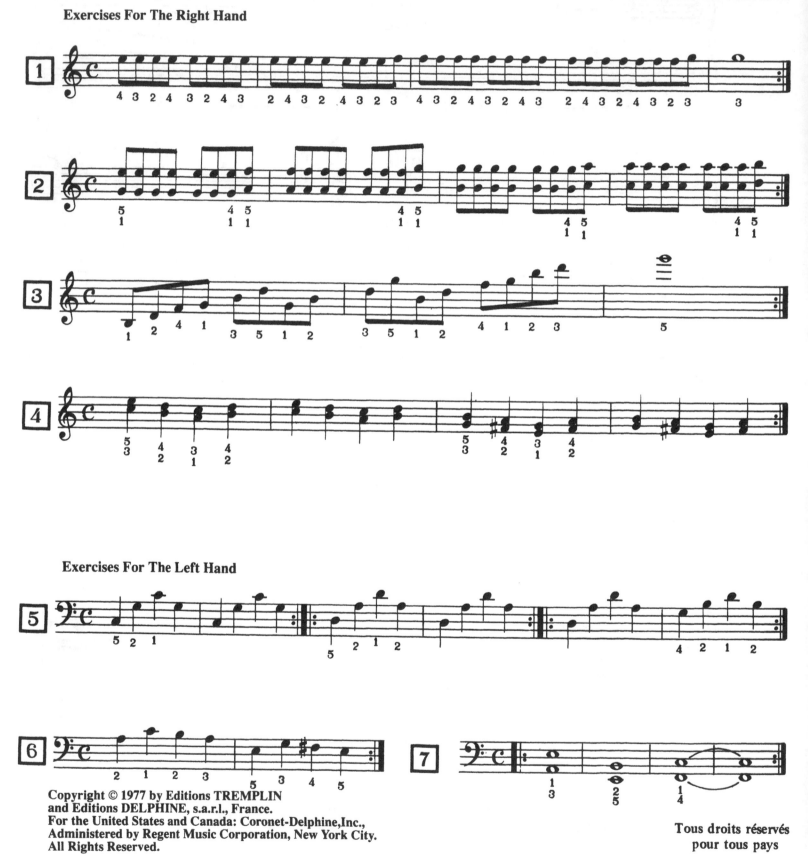

Exercises For The Left Hand

Tous droits réservés
pour tous pays

Lent

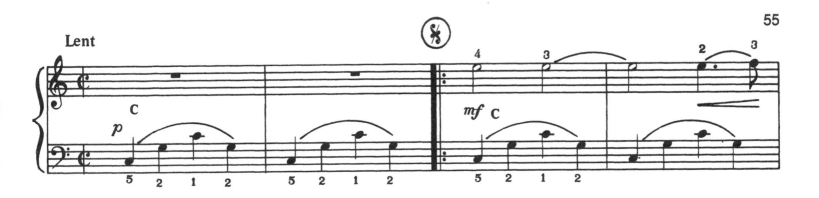

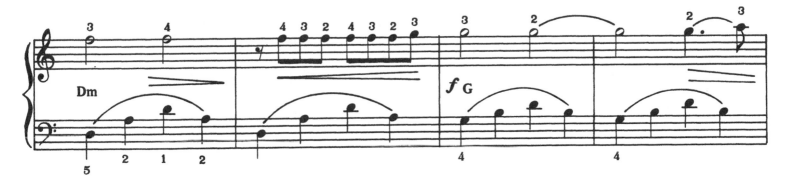

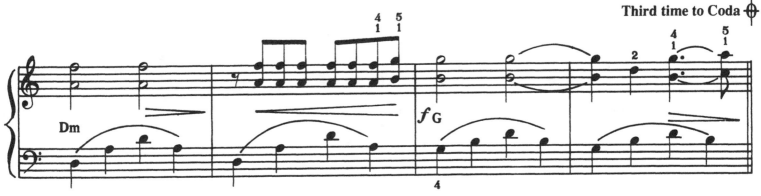

Third time to Coda

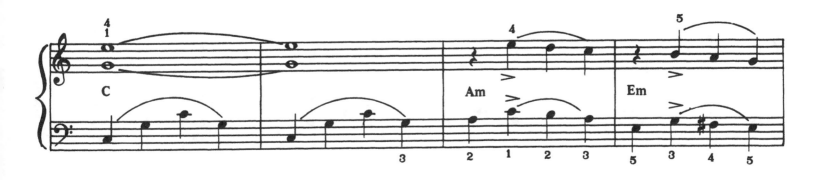

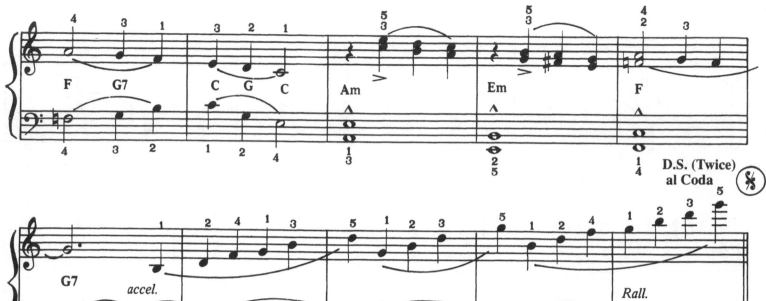

D.S. (Twice)
al Coda

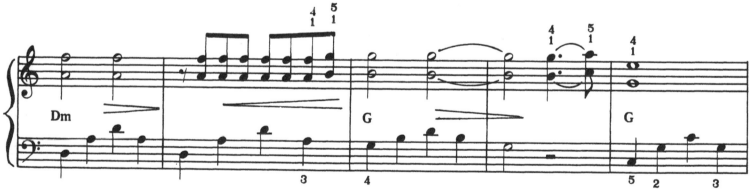

CODA

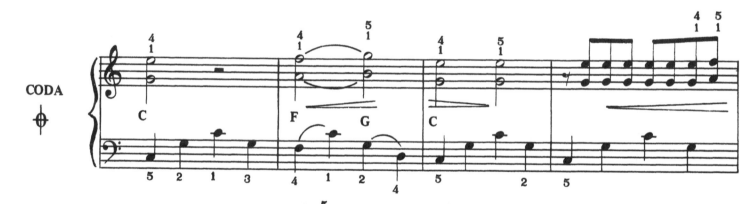

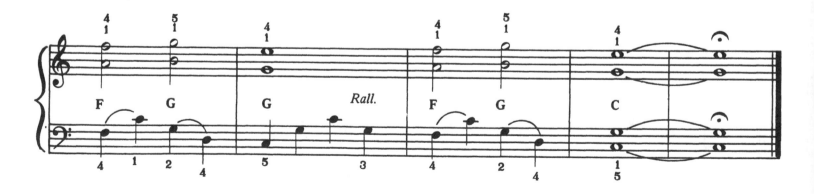

NOSTALGIC MELODIES

Musique de:
Olivier TOUSSAINT

Exercise For The Right Hand

Exercise For The Left Hand

Rock Tempo

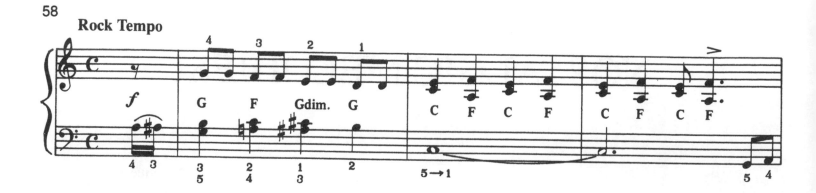

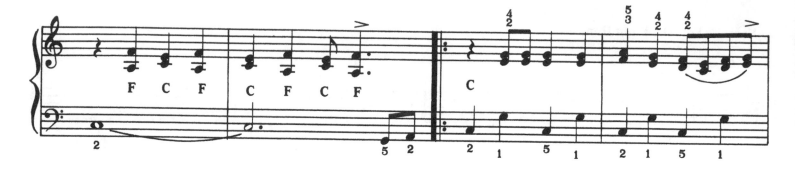

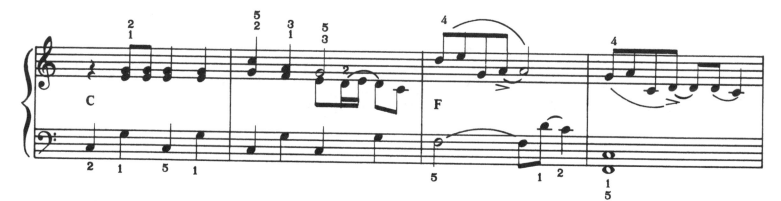

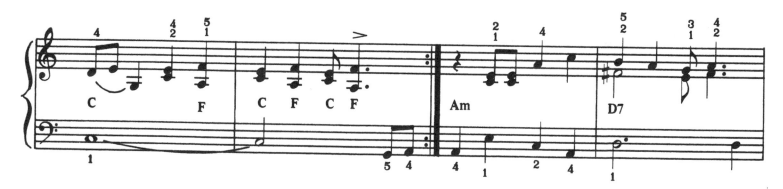

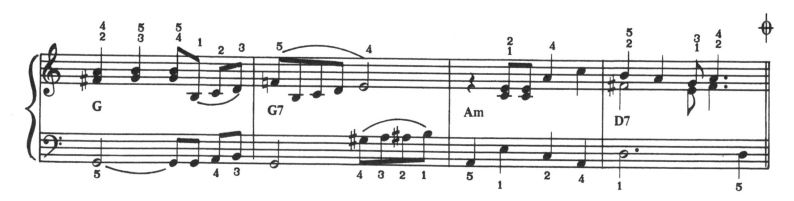

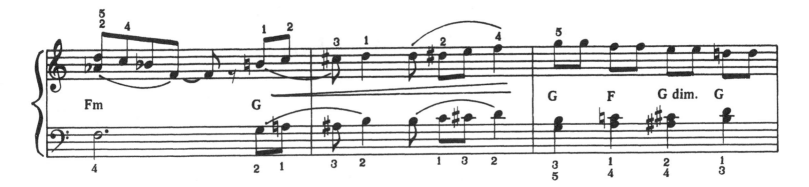

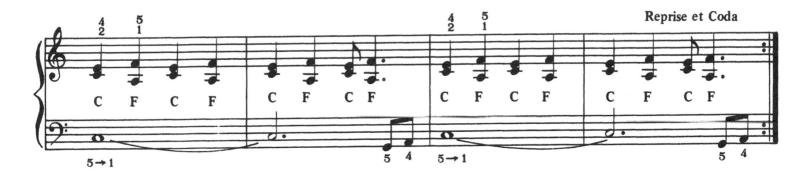

Reprise et Coda

CODA

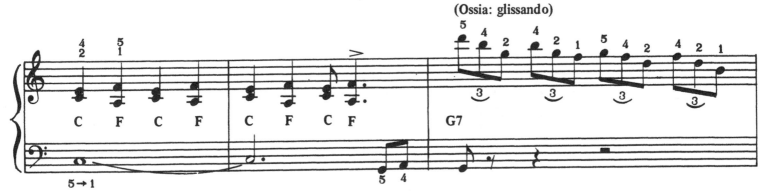

(Ossia: glissando)

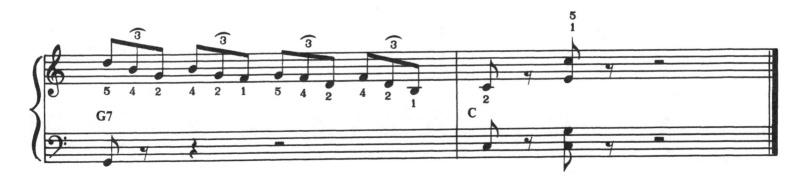

THE LAST DAYS OF ANASTASIA KEMSKY

Musique de: Paul de SENNEVILLE
et Jean BAUDLOT

Exercises For The Right Hand

Exercise For The Left Hand

Moderato

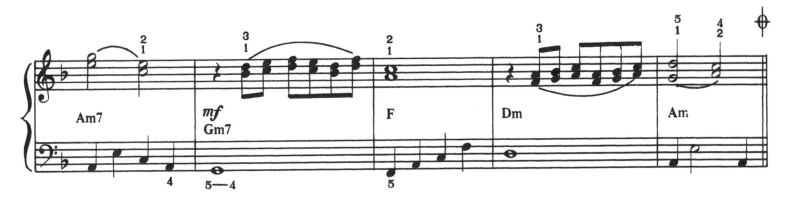

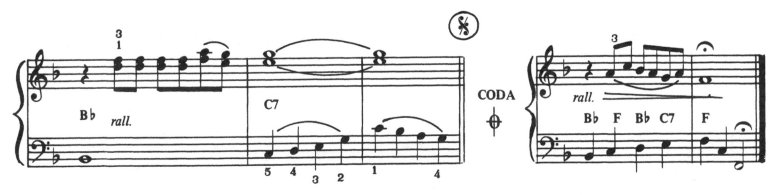

HOPE

Musique de:
Olivier TOUSSAINT

Exercise For The Right Hand

Exercise For The Left Hand

Allegretto

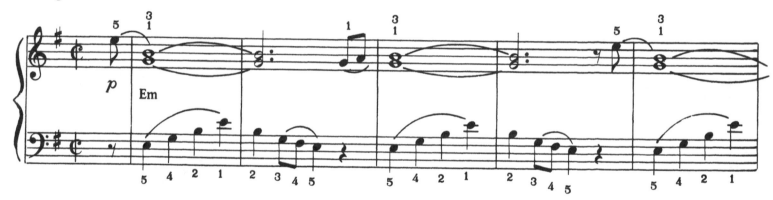

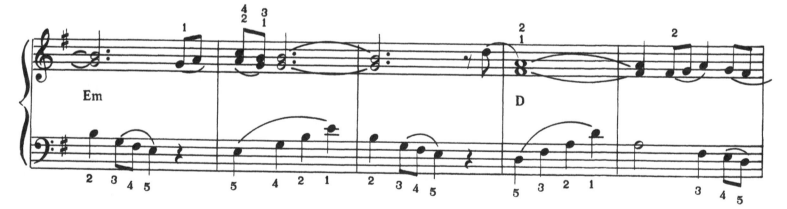

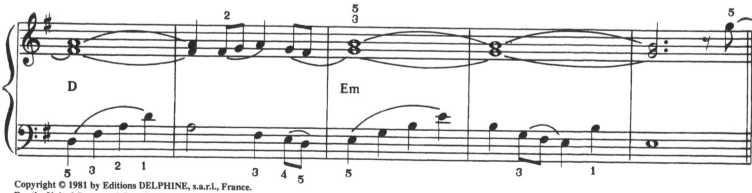

Tous droits réservés
pour tous pays

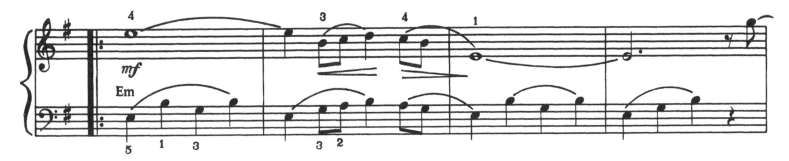

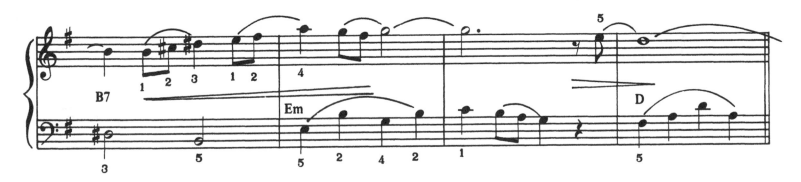

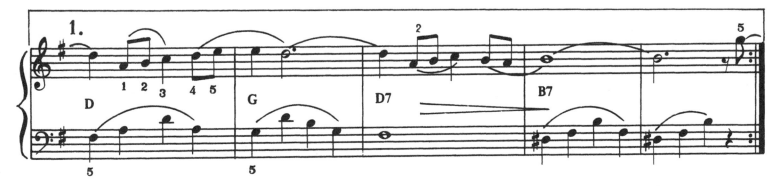

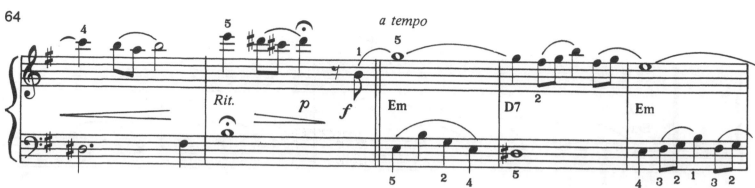

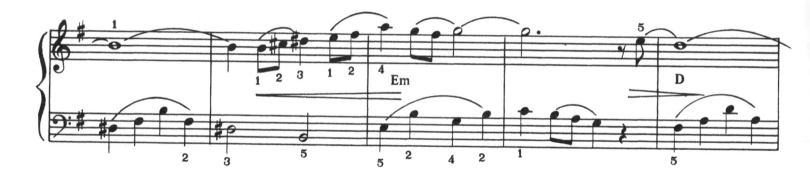

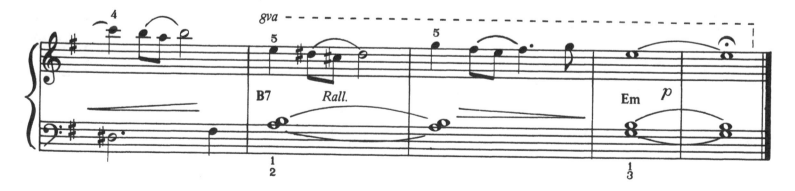